WE OVERCAME!

"This book is dedicated to my parents.

It's through God's grace, and their grace, that I'm able to survive."

-Tomeaka Fladger

Thank you to the creative minds that helped to bring this to life

Sugar Pea Studio

Penwork Publishing

Exquisite Publishing

Thank you for your hard work, professionalism, and believing in me.

This book was inspired by the Negro Spiritual, "We Shall Overcome," by Charles Albert Tindley. Some day is not on the calendar.

Let's define someday!

Someday is…. February 1, 2035

And it is where our story begins.

Our story began fifteen years ago in November 2020. We elected Andrew Yang as The United States of America. He was able to unify the working class through his economic policy on Universal Basic Income (UBI) in which every adult over 18 received $1300 per month [1] with $300 being applied towards one's healthcare

Of course, the government took right it's cut off the top for those who owed back taxes, child support, and student loans. It still left the average adult with at least an additional $500 dollars month that they did not previously. This helped those who were constantly underwater financially begin to breathe.

Previous government assistance programs encouraged the separation of families, but now many families were able to raise their children in stronger, two-parent households. Oftentimes before, with food assistance programs, a two-parent adult household $_2$ would cause a reduction in benefits. Housing assistance program rules even prevented two parents from being in a unified household. Families, in this time, with only one parent with children could often receive more benefits than a household with two working parents. The Universal Basic Income (UBI) Policy did not have income restrictions and as a result, most families embraced the "American Dream," and were able to stay together, on paper and in life.

Previously, poverty was known to be very stressful, Making one feel like they are playing a live version of the game, Twister, with one never having enough limbs to cover all the gaps. Everyone's stress levels came down significantly, and citizens became healthier with the advancement of the UBI policy.

Many adults started their own small businesses, often at home, with the additional monthly income from the UBI policy. Thanks to the internet, people were able to express themselves freely, regardless of age, gender, or race. Many even created businesses dependent upon their own social relationships with others.

The youth did not wait until they turned 16 to find their first job. They created their own financial streams before they hit puberty. Financial literacy and entrepreneurship was woven into the educational system from elementary to high school. All children understood the rules, both written and unwritten, of capitalism and free market economics. With new knowledge and independence, they all began to live by the Wu-Tang Clan's motto of C.R.E.A.M. [3]

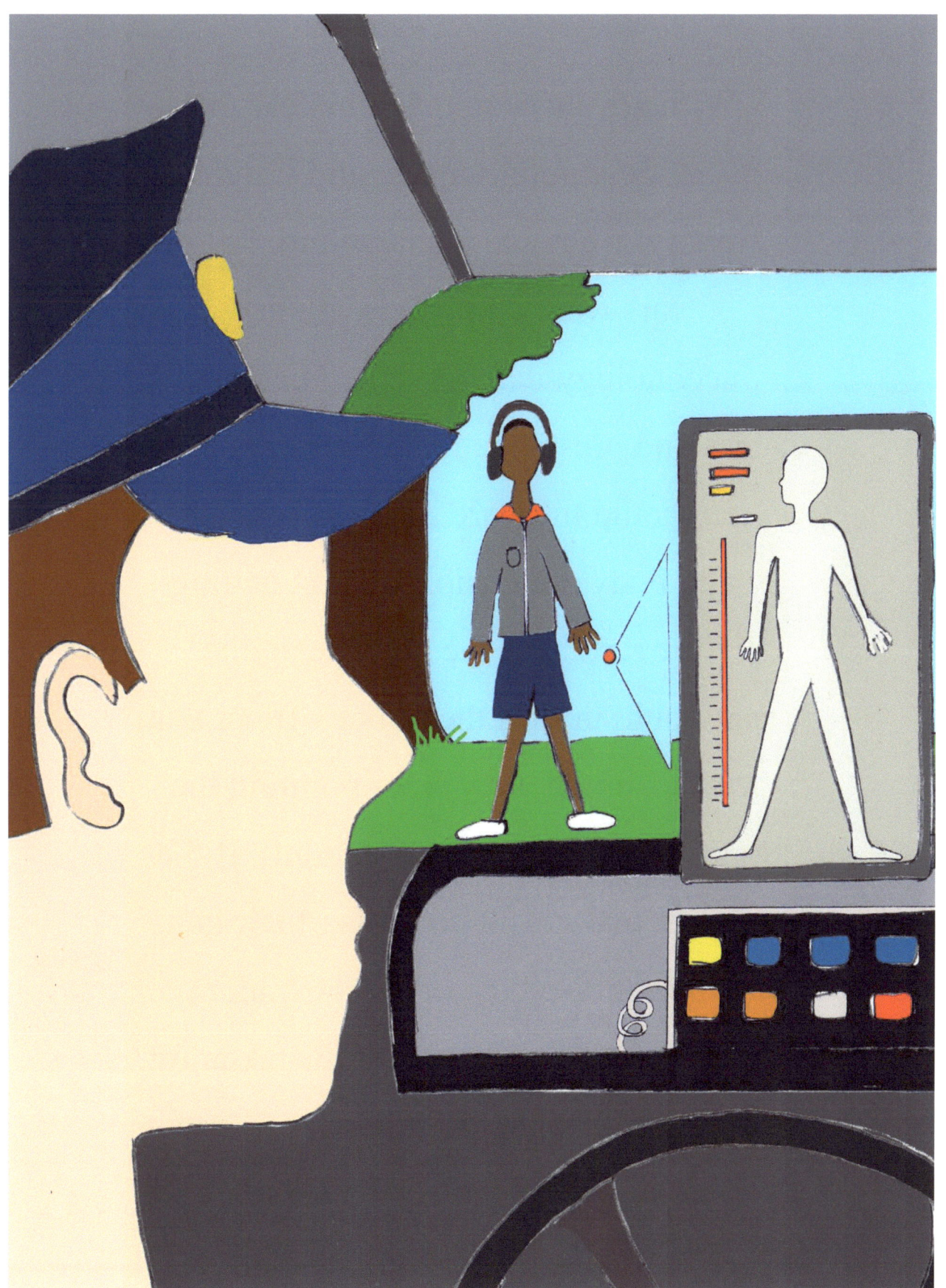

With advances in machine learning, artificial intelligence, and virtual reality, we made justice blind. Police cars were upgraded with new technology that prevented personal bias and pre-judgement. Sensors on the car could measure a person's height and body dimensions. Upon getting the results of the body scan, the car would inform the police officer that, for example, they were pointing the gun at a child, and not an adult, If the police officer did not lower their gun, the car tased the officer. Children playing with toys weren't mistaken for adults with weapons anymore. Parents no longer feared if their children would return home safe and alive.

The steering wheel also doubled as a lie detector. When the officer attempted to put on their lights for a traffic stop, for an unjustified reason, the car would ask the officer why they were stopping the person. If the officer could not justify the reason, the lights and sirens would not turn on. Data was collected on every traffic stop. That data was then transferred, immediately to the officer's commanding officer, as well as an elected Citizens Advisory Board that randomly audited cases on a monthly basis.

In the courts, an Alexa-like
device was used in the jury
room. Anytime a juror came
to a false conclusion,
that was not substantiated by the facts
of the case during the trial,
the Alexa-like device would
correct the mistaken juror,
and inform the jury of what
was truly presented at trial.

Judges did not issue a sentence without submitting their proposed recommendation into an app that housed Millions of previous cases. Upon entering the sentencing recommendation, the app would compare the judge's recommendation with similar cases in the respective state that the crime took place in, or against all federal cases for federal crimes. The app would look for racial bias, and fairness in sentencing. If the sentence recommendation was not fair and consistent, it would throw the judge's sentencing out and make a recommendation that was fair.

An amendment was added to the constitution that prevented men from ever writing laws pertaining to a woman's health without committees consisting of 90% female legislators.

With virtual reality stimulations, ever one had the opportunity to exchange experiences such as: white privilege, being a woman, or being a black male in society. These experiences created more empathy in a society that had long built walls between people and groups. These stimulations created opportunities for groups to have difficult, but necessary, conversations about their different experiences.

WHAT DOES YOUR SOMEDAY LOOK LIKE?

A NOTE FROM THE AUTHOR

I wrote this book as a call to action to my community, we are living in a great time to be alive, yet we don't realize it, With the advent of the internet, social media, and other technology innovations, we have the opportunity to make real change in our community, without waiting on others to suddenly decide that it is time to do the right thing.

We are living in a time where the last thing you want to do is WAIT! we are living in a time where we get to CREATE the world in which we want to live in. It doesn't matter your age, your color, your education level, your zip code, or your criminal background. Will it be harder if you have many of these issues, yes, but not insurmountable. The internet changed the entry point of entrepreneurship. You don't have to have a building to start a business. You can sell t-shirts without even having to house inventory. The question, "what do you want to be when you grow up?" is no longer a question we should ask our children rather we should be asking them what they want to create, and begin to help and support their creation.

Other communities are recognizing and harnessing this moment, and building the world they want to live in. I don't want us to miss this moment in time. I wanted to create a visual book for adults so we can begin to envision what can be, because we are responsible for instilling that vision into our children. It is my hope with this book that we can begin a new conversation in our community about what can be and what we want our community to be. We cannot wait for others to create our vision, nor should we want them to be the sole provider of our vision.

This book illustrates what I would like to see, but I welcome others to add to their vision by joining DPP (Dear Poor People) on our various social media channels.

The social media channels for DPP are:

https://dearpoorpeople.com

https://www.fanbase.app/@DPPSQuad

https://www.facebook.com/DPPSquad?_rdc=2&_rdr

https://www.youtube.com/@dppsquad

REFERENCES

1. Presidential candidate Andrew Yang's policy provides every adult with $1,000 per month. In this version, every adult would get $1,000 before taxes and $300 would be used to pay for healthcare. Presidential candidate Andrew Yang has not endorsed the book.

2. Please note the author is not implying anything is wrong with single parent homes or that people must be married to raise stable children. The author simply means that it takes a village and that children should have access to both parents.

3. "C.R.E.A.M" is the 1993 single from hip-hop group, Wu-Tang Clan. The song title is an acronym for *Cash Rules Everything Around Me*. Since its release the acronym has become popular in hip-hop music and culture.

Greatness Resides Within

https://dearpoorpeople.com